Drawing
Pirates

In this book you will find:

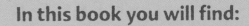

3 pages of hints and tips
to help you draw your best pirates

4 sheets of stickers
to decorate your drawings

8 pages of pirate paper
to help you create pirate clothing,
objects and background scenes

2 pirate stencils
to get you started

40 pages of pirates
to color and decorate

4 pages
of pirate information

Drawing
Pirates

Colored pencils, a pair of scissors and lots of imagination will turn these pages into the most exciting pirates ever!

1 The coloring and drawing pages

Let your imagination run wild! Use the stencils, the special pirate paper and any markers, pencils or crayons you have. And don't forget the stickers!

2 Using the stencils

Use the first page of stencils to draw the pirates.

Then, the second page of stencils will help you give your pirates clothes and weapons.

You can also use the stencils on the second page to add clothes and weapons to the pirates on the drawing pages.

Stencils

Pirate paper

Stickers

Drawing
Pirates

PQW083289

Pirate ships often hid in coves near cliffs so they could take other ships by surprise. On the captain's orders the pirates came from below deck shouting and brandishing their weapons as they boarded the unsuspecting ship. A good pirate had to be strong and mean and know how to use his sword. Each pirate who survived the fight was entitled to a share of the treasure.

The Treasure Hunt

Pirates plundered and stole from as many ships as they could. The stolen booty was shared according to the law of the pirate ship, with the cook getting the smallest share because he didn't fight. Many people say that pirate ship captains buried their treasures in secret locations marked on cryptic maps. Some treasure hunters still look today...

User's Guide

1. Carefully remove the stencils.

2. Pick the pirate stencil you'd like to use first and place it on the background you've chosen (look on the backs of the pirate drawing pages). Or chose one of the pirates who've been drawn for you and use the second page of stencils to dress him and arm him for battle! Use the pirate paper with the stencils to make his clothes look lifelike.

3. Use a pencil to trace the cutout area of the stencil onto the paper. Try to hold the stencil very still.

4. Carefully remove the stencil. Cut out or color what you've drawn.

③ Sticker suggestions

Use the sticker pages to customize and decorate the drawing pages and the pirates you create using the stencils.

Drawing Pirates

 USER'S GUIDE

(4) Pirate Information

At the end of the book you'll find pages filled with pirate information — everything you need to know about pirate life!

Attack!

Special thanks to those who participated in the design and production of *Drawing Pirates*:
Maylis Bellamy-Brown, Jean-Louis Broust, Catherine Changeux, Édouard Leplat, Brigitte Legendre, Laure Maj, Laurence Pasquini, Adèle Pedrola, Roc Prepress, Marjorie Seger, Véronique Sem, Karine Van Wormhoudt, Marie-France Wolfsperger, Marc Goubier (interior illustrations) and Matthieu Roussel (cover design).

First American Edition 2011
Kane Miller, A Division of EDC Publishing
P.O. Box 470663, Tulsa, OK 74147-0663

First published by Editions Play Bac in France in 2010
Copyright © original French version, Editions Play Bac, France 2010
Copyright © American English version, Kane Miller, USA 2011

Manufactured by Regent Publishing Services, Hong Kong
Printed March 2011 in ShenZhen, Guangdong, China
1 2 3 4 5 6 7 8 9 10 • 978-1-61067-057-9

www.kanemiller.com • www.edcpub.com • www.usbornebooksandmore.com

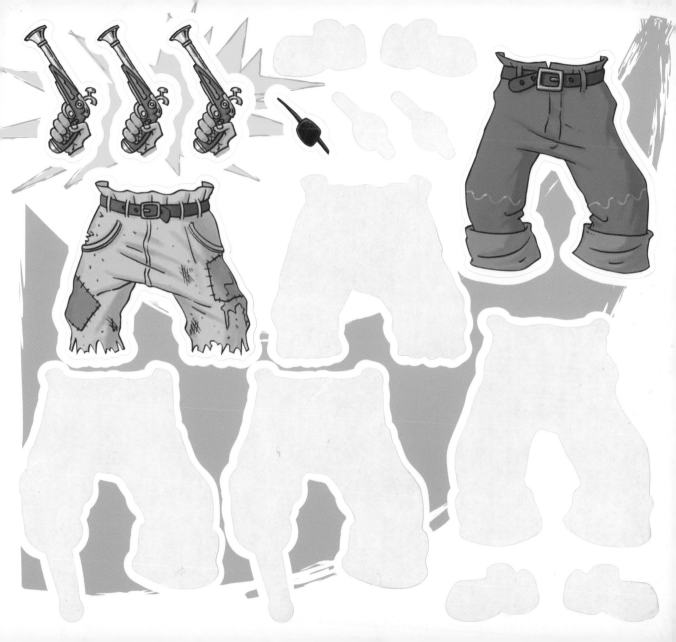

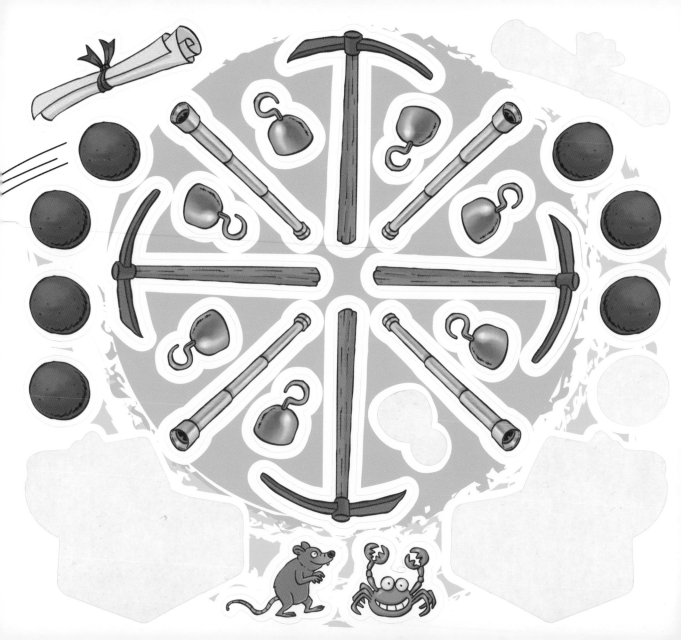

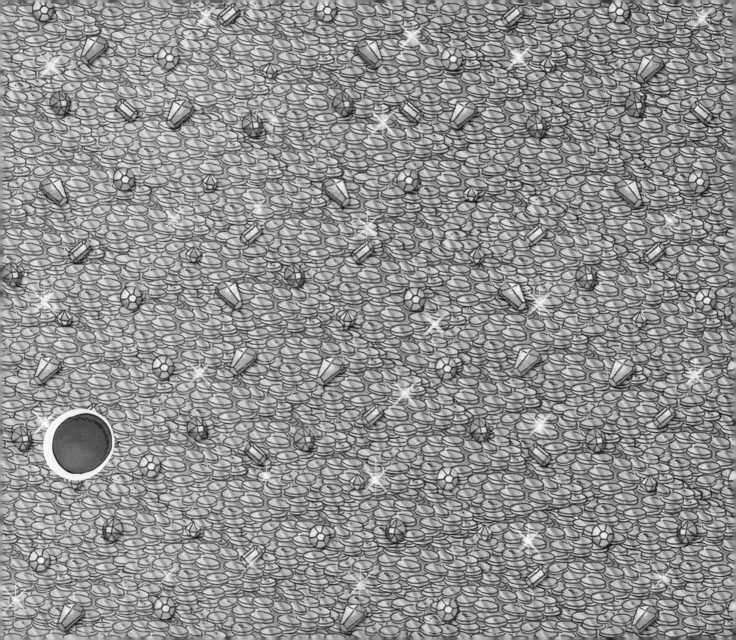

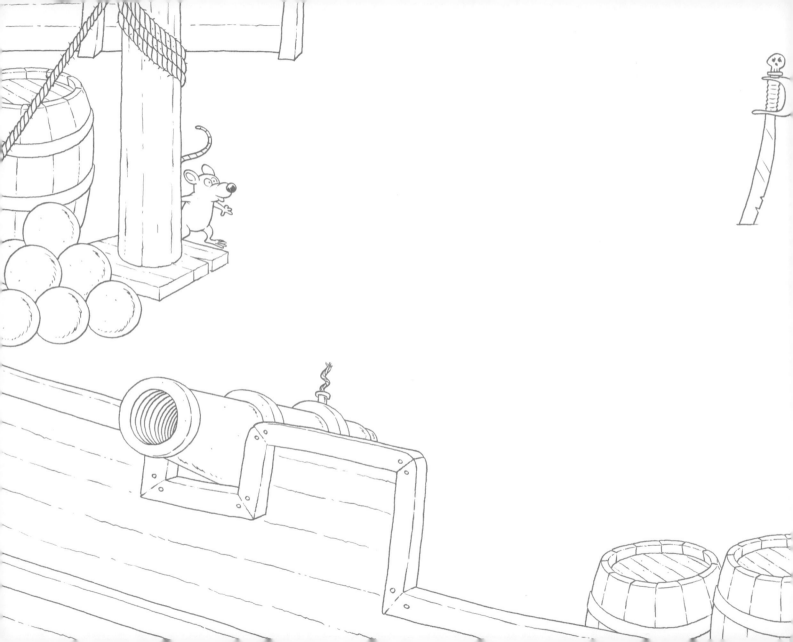

The Black Flag

The pirate flag, black, with a skull and crossbones in the center, is often called the Jolly Roger. Pirates often raised the flag right before they boarded a boat, taking their opponents by surprise and frightening them. They were cruel sea bandits, preying on all ships unlucky enough to come their way.

Life on BoarD

 Life on a pirate ship was hard. Many pirates died from lack of fresh food and water and from diseases brought on board ship by rats. There were chores day and night: cleaning the bridge, standing as lookout, repairing the boat... all the while waiting to attack.